CELEBRITY
TURDS- A CRAPPY
Alphabet Book

LAUREN IRELAND

HIS POOP WEARS BASKETBALL SHORTS, TELLS FART JOKES, AND OCCASIONALLY SINGS IN A WEIRD VOICE WHILE MAKING YOU QUESTION YOUR LIFE CHOICES.

POOP PERSONALITY:
SLACKER COMEDIAN

LOOKS LIKE:
LUMPY AND IRREGULAR, WEARING METAPHORICAL CARGO SHORTS. IT HAS A GOOFY SMILE, AND SOMEHOW IT'S PLAYING A KAZOO.

GLITTERY, PERFECTLY FORMED, AND SOMEHOW IN FORMATION. SMELLS LIKE SASHA FIERCE AND CONFIDENCE.

POOP PERSONALITY:
FLAWLESS QUEEN

LOOKS LIKE:
PERFECTLY SCULPTED, GOLD-DUSTED, WITH A SPARKLY SHIMMER. WHEN THE LIGHT HITS IT RIGHT, IT PRACTICALLY SINGS "HALO."

B – BEYONCÉ

LOOKS LIKE A DINO NUGGET.
USED TO BE GOOFY AND
HARMLESS, BUT NOW IT HITS
THE BOWL LIKE A BLOCKBUSTER
ACTION SEQUENCE.

POOP PERSONALITY:
FROM CHUBBY GOOFBALL TO
ACTION HERO

LOOKS LIKE:
LIKE IT JUST ESCAPED JURASSIC
PARK — A CHUNKY TURD WITH
A RAPTOR CLAW EMBEDDED IN
IT. SURPRISINGLY FIT.

C – CHRIS PRATT

AN UNPREDICTABLE, ODDLY
COIFFED MASS THAT ARRIVES
WITH FANFARE AND INSISTS IT
BROKE ALL PREVIOUS POOP
RECORDS. DEMANDS A GOLDEN
TOILET JUST TO FEEL AT HOME

POOP PERSONALITY:
BOASTFUL, DEFIANT.

LOOKS LIKE:
A VAGUELY ORANGE SWIRL WITH
AN UNNATURAL SHINE

D – DONALD TRUMP

TECHNICALLY SOUTH AFRICAN-BORN, BUT LIVES IN THE U.S. NOW. HIS POOP WANTS TO COLONIZE MARS, TWEETS WHILE FLUSHING, AND EXPLODES UNPREDICTABLY.

POOP PERSONALITY:
ECCENTRIC TECH MOGUL

LOOKS LIKE:
METALLIC, VAGUELY SHAPED LIKE A TESLA LOGO. GLOWS FAINTLY. YOU'RE AFRAID TO FLUSH IT — IT MIGHT LAUNCH.★

CHARMING BUT TOTALLY
FORGETTABLE — YOU'D SWEAR
IT WAS THERE, BUT NOW IT'S
GONE AND NO ONE TALKS
ABOUT IT.

POOP PERSONALITY:
2000S TEEN DREAM

LOOKS LIKE:
SOFT, HANDSOME, AND
SURPRISINGLY SYMMETRICAL.
YOU KIND OF MISS IT WHEN
IT'S GONE.

F – FREDDIE PRINZE JR.

SMELLS LIKE HARAJUKU PERFUME AND LOOKS LIKE IT'S BEEN DIP-DYED IN PINK. OCCASIONALLY YELLS "THIS SH*T IS BANANAS. B-A-N-A-N-A-S!"

POOP PERSONALITY:
2000S POP ICON MEETS PUNK

LOOKS LIKE:
NEON PINK AND BLACK STRIPES, WITH A TINY CHAIN WALLET. SMELLS LIKE BUBBLEGUM AND REBELLION.

G – GWEN STEFANI

OKAY, HE'S AUSTRALIAN, BUT AMERICANS CLAIM HIM. HIS POOP STARTS AS A CLASSY BROADWAY NUMBER, THEN CLAWS ITS WAY OUT IN FULL WOLVERINE RAGE MODE.

POOP PERSONALITY:
MUSICAL WOLVERINE

LOOKS LIKE:
A CLASSY, TUXEDO-WEARING LOG WITH ADAMANTIUM CLAWS POKING OUT. STARTS SINGING "THE GREATEST SHOW" AS IT SPIRALS.

H – HUGH JACKMAN

COLD, HARD, AND NARRATES ITS OWN EXIT LIKE A GRITTY POLICE DRAMA. "YOU THOUGHT IT WAS OVER... BUT THE REAL CRIME IS WHAT'S COMING."

POOP PERSONALITY:
OG MEETS LAW & ORDER

LOOKS LIKE:
COLD, HARD, LIKE A FROZEN SNICKERS BAR WEARING SUNGLASSES. ONE EYEBROW RAISED LIKE IT KNOWS YOU DID SOMETHING WRONG.

AN ABSOLUTE UNIT OF A TURD WITH A SIX-PACK AND TRIBAL TATTOOS. IT FLEXES BEFORE IT FLUSHES, CALLS YOU "BRO," AND SOMEHOW FLIRTS WITH YOUR TOILET BEFORE RESPECTFULLY DISAPPEARING

POOP PERSONALITY:
CHILL, ECO-FRIENDLY

LOOKS LIKE:
A BRAIDED LOG CARVED FROM MAHOGANY WITH MUSCLES

J – JASON MOMOA

PERFECTLY SHAPED. BREAKS THE TOILET LIKE SHE BROKE THE INTERNET. PROBABLY FILTERED ON INSTAGRAM BEFORE YOU EVEN FLUSHED.

POOP PERSONALITY:
SCULPTED AND GLAM

LOOKS LIKE:
SHAPED LIKE A PERFECTLY CONTOURED PEACH EMOJI. IT'S WEARING HIGHLIGHTER AND SOMEHOW FILTERED IN REAL LIFE.

DRY, NEUROTIC, AND SHAPED LIKE A QUESTION MARK. COMPLAINS THE WHOLE WAY OUT AND SOMEHOW STILL BLAMES THE PLUMBING.

POOP PERSONALITY:
CRANKY AND CONFUSED

LOOKS LIKE:
THIN, SPIRALED, NERVOUSLY COILED IN ON ITSELF. COMPLAINS MID-FLUSH ABOUT THE TEMPERATURE OF THE TOILET SEAT.

NARRATES ITS OWN JOURNEY FROM INTESTINE TO BOWL WITH MAJESTIC GRAVITAS. YOU CRY A LITTLE. IT'S ART.

POOP PERSONALITY:
WISE NARRATOR OF EXISTENCE

LOOKS LIKE:
A DIGNIFIED, SLOW-MOVING SWIRL THAT LOOKS YOU IN THE EYES AND WHISPERS, "THIS... IS THE END OF A LONG JOURNEY."

YOU NEVER KNOW WHAT YOU'RE GONNA GET — COULD BE A MASTERPIECE, COULD BE A FLAMING DISASTER. EITHER WAY, IT STARES BACK AT YOU INTENSELY.

POOP PERSONALITY: UNPREDICTABLE CHAOS

LOOKS LIKE:
WILD-EYED AND FLAMING, CHANGES SHAPE MID-FALL. SOMETIMES IT'S A NICOLAS CAGE FACE. NO ONE KNOWS WHY.

N - NICOLAS CAGE

GENEROUS, DRAMATIC, AND COMES WITH FREE GIFTS. "YOU GET A POOP! AND YOU GET A POOP!"

POOP PERSONALITY:
GENEROUS ICON

LOOKS LIKE:
BIG, BOLD, GOLD-FLECKED, AND OPRAH-SHAPED. WHEN IT DROPS, IT YELLS "EVERYBODY POOPS!"

TATTED, MESSY, AND SMELLS
LIKE BEER AND BACKSTAGE.
LEAVES BEHIND A MYSTERY
AND MAYBE SOME GLITTER.

POOP PERSONALITY:
MESSY BUT LOVABLE

LOOKS LIKE:
COVERED IN TATTOOS,
HALF-MELTED, AND SMELLS
LIKE BEER AND FEBREZE. IT
WINKS AT YOU

P - POST MALONE

WAY TOO LONG. WEIRDLY
STYLISH. HAS A FOOT IN IT FOR
SOME REASON

POOP PERSONALITY:
STYLISH WEIRDO WITH A FOOT
THING

LOOKS LIKE:
BRIGHT RED, DRAMATIC
ANGLES, AND A TINY DOLL
FOOT POKING OUT. SOMEHOW
IT'S IN SLOW MOTION.

Q – QUENTIN TARANTINO

SHINY, FABULOUS, AND LEAVES A TRAIL OF SEQUINS. STRUTS DOWN THE BOWL LIKE A RUNWAY. "SASHAY AWAY."

POOP PERSONALITY:
GLAMOROUS, FIERCE, ICONIC

LOOKS LIKE:
A SPARKLING TURD IN STILETTOS. WEARS A TINY WIG AND SAYS, "IF YOU CAN'T LOVE YOUR POOP, HOW THE HELL YOU GONNA LOVE SOMEBODY ELSE?"

R - RUPAUL

LOUD, ANGRY, AND FULL OF PROFANITY. SAYS "I'VE HAD IT WITH THESE MOTHERFIN' TURDS IN THIS MOTHERFIN' BOWL!"

POOP PERSONALITY:
ANGRY, LOUD, INTENSE

LOOKS LIKE:
A HARD, STEAMING COIL THAT SLAMS INTO THE BOWL WITH ATTITUDE AND SAYS "FLUSH ME ONE MORE TIME, MOTHERF***ER!"

S - SAMUEL L. JACKSON

NEATLY SHAPED, LEAVES A BREAKUP MESSAGE ON THE TOILET PAPER, AND SOMEHOW BECOMES A CHART-TOPPING HIT.

POOP PERSONALITY:
BREAKUP SONG IN FECAL FORM

LOOKS LIKE:
NEAT AND PASTEL-COLORED. LEAVES BEHIND GLITTER AND A STICKY NOTE THAT SAYS, "WE ARE NEVER EVER GETTING BACK TOGETHER."

T- TAYLOR SWIFT

SMOOTH, SMELLS LIKE COLOGNE, AND MOONWALKS INTO THE BOWL WHISPERING "YEAH!" IN FALSETTO.

POOP PERSONALITY:
SMOOTH AND SENSUAL

LOOKS LIKE:
A SILKY, PERFECTLY CURVED LOG WITH COLOGNE MIST WAFTING UP. SLIDES OUT TO A SLOW JAM BEAT.

U – USHER

THICK, DIESEL-FUELED, AND ALL ABOUT "FAMILY." GROWLS AS IT EXITS.

POOP PERSONALITY:
FAST & FURIOUS

LOOKS LIKE:
BUILT LIKE A BRICK, COMES OUT IN SLOW MOTION WHILE SHOUTING "FAMILY!" SOUNDS LIKE A MUSCLE CAR ENGINE.

V – VIN DIESEL

WISE, WARM, AND A LITTLE SARCASTIC. PROBABLY WEARS LITTLE GLASSES AND GIVES YOU LIFE ADVICE MID-FLUSH.

POOP PERSONALITY:
WISE, SARCASTIC, WARM

LOOKS LIKE:
A NO-NONSENSE, TEXTURED LOG WITH DREADLOCKS MADE OF TOILET PAPER. IT DROPS WITH A QUIP ABOUT YOUR FIBER INTAKE.

W - WHOOPI GOLDBERG

"YO DAWG, I HEARD YOU LIKE FLUSHING, SO I PUT A TOILET IN YOUR TOILET SO YOU CAN POOP WHILE YOU POOP."

POOP PERSONALITY:
PIMP MY POOP

LOOKS LIKE:
A TURD INSIDE A TINY GOLD-PLATED TOILET, WHICH IS INSIDE A LARGER TURD. "YO DAWG, I HEARD YOU LIKE LAYERS…"

X - XZIBIT

UNAPOLOGETIC, GROUNDBREAKING, AND CONVINCED IT'S REDEFINING THE ENTIRE BATHROOM EXPERIENCE.

POOP PERSONALITY:
CONFIDENT, MISUNDERSTOOD, AND INSISTS IT SHOULD HEADLINE COACHELLA INSTEAD OF GOING DOWN THE DRAIN.

LOOKS LIKE:
SCULPTURAL, YEEZY-TONED MASS WITH FUTURISTIC ANGLES

QUIRKY, SHAPED LIKE A UKULELE, AND WEARS VINTAGE GLASSES. PROBABLY HUMS AN INDIE TUNE AS IT GOES DOWN.

POOP PERSONALITY:
QUIRKY AND ADORABLE

LOOKS LIKE:
POLKA-DOTTED, SHAPED LIKE A UKULELE, WEARS FAKE LASHES. LEAVES BEHIND A POST-IT NOTE POEM AND A LAVENDER SPRITZ.

Z - ZOOEY DESCHANEL

THE
END

www.ingramcontent.com/pod-product-compliance
Lightning Source LLC
Chambersburg PA
CBHW071443210326

41597CB00020B/3929